King Cobra

By Audry Graham

Gareth Stevens
Publishing

Please visit our Web site, www.garethstevens.com. For a free color catalog of all our high-quality books, call toll free 1-800-542-2595 or fax 1-877-542-2596.

Library of Congress Cataloging-in-Publication Data

Graham, Audry.
King cobra / Audry Graham.
      p. cm. — (Killer snakes)
ISBN 978-1-4339-4554-0 (pbk.)
ISBN 978-1-4339-4555-7 (6-pack)
ISBN 978-1-4339-4553-3 (library binding)
1. King cobra—Juvenile literature. I. Title.
QL666.O64G73 2011
597.96'42—dc22

                                        2010030696

First Edition

Published in 2011 by
Gareth Stevens Publishing
111 East 14th Street, Suite 349
New York, NY 10003

Designer: Michael J. Flynn
Editor: Greg Roza

Photo credits: Cover, pp. 1, (2–4, 6, 8, 10, 12, 14, 16, 18, 20–24 snake skin texture), 5, 7, 11, 15 (main image), 21 Shutterstock.com; p. 9 Joe McDonald/Visuals Unlimited/Getty Images; p. 13 iStockphoto.com; pp. 15 (fangs and venom), 19 Mattias Klum/National Geographic/Getty Images; p. 17 ZSSD/Minden Pictures/Getty Images.

Printed in the United States of America

CPSIA compliance information: Batch #CW11GS: For further information contact Gareth Stevens, New York, New York at 1-800-542-2595.

Contents

Boldface words appear in the glossary.

King of the Cobras

The king cobra is the longest **venomous** snake in the world! They can grow up to 18 feet (5.5 m) long and weigh up to 20 pounds (9 kg). Their venom is deadly. One king cobra bite has enough venom to kill an elephant!

5

King Cobras at Home

King cobras are found in Southeast Asia and parts of India. They live in wooded places and open plains. King cobras can be light brown, dark brown, or greenish-brown. They may have white, brown, or yellow stripes. Their bellies are yellow or white.

Asia

KEY

king cobra

In the Nest

Female king cobras lay between 20 and 50 eggs at one time. They are the only snakes that make nests for their eggs. The adult king cobra keeps the eggs safe until the babies **hatch** about 60 to 90 days later. Each baby is about 20 inches (51 cm) long.

9

Stay Away!

The king cobra is easily angered. It **attacks** quickly when it is surprised. Sudden movements make it strike, too. When a king cobra is scared or angry, it flattens its neck and spreads it out to make itself look bigger. This is called a hood.

hood

11

The king cobra has short **fangs**. To make up for this, it raises its head up to 5 feet (1.5 m) off the ground. Then it brings its head down quickly and drives its fangs into its enemy. It can also strike from 7 feet (2.1 m) away!

13

King Cobra Venom

King cobra venom isn't very strong compared to other snake venom. However, a king cobra bite has much more venom in it than the bites of other venomous snakes. This makes it one of the deadliest snakes in the world.

fangs and venom

15

On the Hunt

The king cobra hunts mainly during the day. It eats mostly other snakes. Some also eat lizards, eggs, and small **mammals**. King cobras don't spread their hoods or rise up when attacking **prey**. These actions are just a warning for their enemies.

A king cobra uses its tongue to smell its prey. It also has excellent eyesight. It can see prey 300 feet (91 m) away. The king cobra attacks quickly. Its venom **stuns** or kills the prey. Then the king cobra eats the prey whole.

People and King Cobras

King cobras don't like to be around people. This is good for people! Very few people die from king cobra bites each year. However, king cobras attack people when they're scared, surprised, or have no way to escape. One bite can kill a person in just 15 minutes!

Snake Facts
King Cobra

Length	up to 18 feet (5.5 m) long
Weight	up to 20 pounds (9 kg)
Where It Lives	Southeast Asia and parts of India
Life Span	about 20 years
Killer Fact	King cobras sway from side to side as their enemy moves. This is one reason why **snake charmers** use them in their acts. Most king cobra bites happen to snake charmers!

Glossary

attack: to try to harm someone or something

fang: a sharp tooth

hatch: to break out of an egg

mammal: an animal that has live young and feeds them milk from the mother's body

prey: an animal hunted by other animals for food

snake charmer: someone who handles snakes and dances to music with them

stun: to shock something so it can't move

venomous: able to produce a liquid called venom that is harmful to other animals

For More Information

Books

Mattern, Joanne. *King Cobras.* Mankato, MN: Capstone Press, 2010.

White, Nancy. *King Cobras: The Biggest Venomous Snakes of All!* New York, NY: Bearport Publishing, 2009.

Web Sites

King Cobra
animals.nationalgeographic.com/animals/reptiles/king-cobra/
Read more about the king cobra.

King Cobras Lock Horns
animal.discovery.com/videos/king-cobra-and-i-cobras-lock-horns.html
Watch a video of two king cobras fighting. Also includes links to other king cobra videos.

Index